The Itty-Bitty Book

of

Financial Affirmations

By

Anita R. Johnson
Financial Behaviorist

The Itty-Bitty Book of Financial Affirmations

Copyright © 2017 Anita R. Johnson

All Rights Reserved.

Cover photo from morguefile.com

No part of this book may be reproduced, stored in a retrieval system, or transmitted by any other means without the written permission of the publisher.

The information in this book is distributed on an "as is" basis without warranty. While every precaution has been taken in the preparation of this book, the author shall not have any liability to any person or entity with respect to any loss or damage caused or alleged to be caused directly or indirectly by the instructions contained in this book.

1. Financial Psychology
2. Motivation

ISBN-13: 978-1545213544

ISBN-10: 1545213542

Dedication

The Itty-Bitty Book of Financial Affirmations is dedicated to my granddaughter Hannah K Beasley.

Uma Loves You

This book belongs to

_____

My goal is to

_____

Signature

Table of Contents

Dedication 4
My goal. 5
Introduction 9
How to Use This Book 10
Summary 21
About the Author 22

Introduction

Finances are very personal. Most people are embarrassed to discuss money with anyone. It is assumed that as you become an adult you will automatically know how to handle your finances. Not true.

A lot of what you know about money, you learned from your guardians, community, religious beliefs, and your personal mindset towards money. This book addresses your money mindset. It gives you a head start on setting positive affirmations.

How to Use This Book

It is important that you learn to create your own financial affirmations and develop the habit of using them each day. I write my affirmation inside my journal every day.

"Money flows to me easily and effortlessly from unexpected resources."

Read each affirmation listed. Think about how you can apply it. Write it down. Then try to make one of your own.

Creating a positive money mindset will guide you to finding your Financial Voice.

☙

Financial Mindset + Financial Knowledge + Financial Power =

Your Financial Voice

Money is a tool used to get from point A to point B, but will not rule me.

To find my financial voice I must change my money mindset. I will think, speak and practice my positive money mindset.

ಙ

I have everything I need and more to pay all bills, to invest in my future for myself and my children.

☙

I will leave a legacy for three generations.

ଚ

I am creating financial abundance.

☙

It's my job as a parent to teach my children how to handle, think and live their financial lives.

Financial setbacks happen. I will learn from them and use them as setups for financial successes.

☙

I will develop a healthy relationship with money.

ಬಂ

I will continue to grow my financial garden with knowledge, professional help, a financial plan and a money mindset.

Summary

The Itty-Bitty Book of Financial Affirmations is the beginning of your financial transformation. Take these affirmations/quotes, build your own financial affirmations. Building your own affirmations will get through the days when money is not easily available. Being in a bad place about money happens each person. Having affirmations helps you focus on the positive and your will to Find Your Financial Voice.

About the Author

Anita R. Johnson is a Financial Behaviorist and author. Anita takes a holistic approach to money; focusing on enhancing your financial well-being, while helping you to understand your emotional behavior around money. Anita knows once a client understands their anxiety around money, he/she can make clear and concise money decisions that will have a positive effect on the legacy they leave.

Contact Information:
Anita R Johnson
Financial Behaviorist, Best Selling Author, Co-Founder of Affluence Financial Fitness for Women

3104 O Street Suite 315
Sacramento CA 95817
915-572-9033

www.anitarjohnson.com
anitafinancialpsychologist@gmail.com

www.ingramcontent.com/pod-product-compliance
Lightning Source LLC
Chambersburg PA
CBHW070720210526
45170CB00021B/1385